Leaves fall just before Halloween

Halloween

Steve Potts

A⁺

Smart Apple Media

Published by Smart Apple Media

1980 Lookout Drive, North Mankato, MN 56003

Designed by Rita Marshall

Printed in the United States of America

Photographs by Roy Gumpel

Library of Congress Cataloging-in-Publication Data

Potts, Steve. Halloween / by Steve Potts. p. cm. – (Holidays series)

Includes bibliographical references and index.

ISBN 1-58340-120-2

1. Halloween–Juvenile literature. [1. Halloween. 2. Holidays.] I. Title.

GT4965 .P68 2001   394.2646–dc21   00-067905

First Edition 9 8 7 6 5 4 3 2 1

COPYRIGHT

Halloween

All Hallows' Eve   6

Halloween Spirits   12

Images of Halloween   14

Trick or Treat   18

Hands On: Halloween Activity   22

Additional Information   24

CONTENTS

All Hallows' Eve

At the very end of October every year, many people around the world celebrate a special day. They dress up in costumes and walk from house to house, calling out, "Trick or treat!" What began as an ancient religious celebration is now known as Halloween. But how did it happen? Of all the special days that people celebrate, Halloween has one of the longest histories. Around the first century, **Celts** celebrated the last day of the Celtic year, October 31, with feasting

Halloween festivities usually begin at dusk

and dancing. 🧹 At the same time, Christians celebrated the

hallowed All Saints' Day on November 1. During the Middle

Ages, these two traditions combined to become All Hallows'

Day on November 1, which made the night **Ancient Celtic history says October 31 is a "day off" for tormented souls.**

before All Hallows' *Eve*. While November 1 is

still celebrated today as All Saints' Day, the

night before eventually came to be known

as Halloween. 🧹 More than 2,000 years ago, it became

customary to dress up in costumes to celebrate October 31.

Celtic Irish priests, called Druids, believed that ghosts and

witches came out to hurt people on this night. The Celts

believed that by wearing costumes they could frighten away

the ghosts or at least confuse them.

Costumes were meant to confuse the spirits

Many people dress up as ghosts

Halloween Spirits

It also became traditional to put out the fires in fireplaces to make homes cold. People believed that ghosts and spirits would not stay in a cold house. Then, all the villagers gathered outside the village and lit a huge **bonfire**. This fire was supposed to drive away evil spirits. Another aspect of the celebration was the end of the harvest. Both the Celts and the Christians who later came to Ireland celebrated the season by giving thanks for their crops. Slowly, All Hallows' Eve became less a night to fear the dead and more a night to

celebrate the season and have fun. In the 1840s, a horri-

ble **famine** occurred in Ireland and many people starved to

death. While hundreds of thousands of people died, many

Picking the right pumpkin to carve

who survived fled to North America. These Irish **immigrants**

brought their Halloween traditions with them and helped

create new ones. The Irish liked to play pranks on

Halloween. They turned over outhouses, took gates off fences,

and played other jokes. This is why Halloween is sometimes

called "mischief night."

Images of Halloween

True to the custom of harvest celebration, Irish settlers

made multicolored corn, called Indian corn, a part of their

Halloween decorating. They also included corn stalks, scare-

crows, and harvest tools such as scythes and pitchforks.

One Irish Halloween custom was slightly changed by the

immigrants who came to North America. In Ireland, scary faces

A one-eyed pirate costume

were carved into large turnips. The turnip was then hollowed out and a burning candle was put inside it. This glowing vegetable was called a jack-o'-lantern. When the Irish came to North America, they replaced the turnip with the pumpkin. Today, people still carve frightening or funny faces into pumpkins. They also put candles in hollow pumpkins that are then set in windows or on front steps. According to an ancient legend, people who had done evil while they were

After the jack-o'-lantern is carved, its seeds can be baked, salted, and eaten.

Jack-o'-lanterns can be funny or scary

alive became cats when they died. That is why black cats are a part of Halloween's scary celebrations.

Trick or Treat

Trick or treat is another ancient custom that is still part of today's Halloween festivities. In the 800s, Christians in Europe went out on All Hallows' Day, also called All Souls' Day, to visit their neighbors. At each house, they asked for biscuits called soul cakes. If someone gave them soul cakes, they had to promise to say a prayer for the person's dead relatives. The more cakes they received, the more prayers they

had to say. This practice was called "souling" because it hap-

pened on All Souls' Day. This practice continued as part of the

All Hallows' Eve festivities. Today, many people still go

In costume and ready to trick-or-treat

trick-or-treating and carve pumpkins, but they do not fear

witches, ghosts, and goblins. The old ideas about Halloween

changed when the Irish came to North **Linking the**
haunted
America. Halloween, October 31, is a day **house to**
Halloween
to go to parties, decorate houses in orange **began in**
England in the
and black, wear funny or scary costumes, and **early 1800s.**

play games, such as bobbing for apples or hide-and-seek.

Halloween is a fun celebration!

A moon mask made of papier-mâché

Halloween Activity

Decorating for Halloween can be just as much fun as costume parties and trick-or-treating. These scary spiders are easy to make and hang on your porch or in your windows.

What You Need

Paper plates (two for each spider)
Black construction paper
Black paint
A paintbrush
Old newspapers

What You Do

Cover your work space with the old newspapers. Cut the construction paper into eight long strips and one circle (for the spider's legs and head). Glue the two paper plates together, top to top, with the legs and head placed between them. Bend the legs so the spider has "knees." Paint the body black. Glue a long piece of string to the middle of the spider's back. Once the spider is dry, it will be ready to dangle at unsuspecting people walking by!

Making masks is as fun as wearing them

Index

All Hallows' Day 8, 18

All Hallows' Eve 8, 12, 19

All Saints' Day 8

All Souls' Day 18–19

Celts 6, 8–9, 12

costumes 6, 8–9, 20

jack-o'-lanterns 16

pranks 14

trick or treat 6, 18–20

Words to Know

bonfire—a large mound of wood and other items that is burned outdoors, usually in celebration or protest

Celts—a group of ancient people who lived in the British Isles

famine—a shortage of food for an extended period of time

hallowed—something that is holy

immigrants—people who permanently move from one country to another

Read More

Chambers, Catherine. *All Saints, All Souls, and Halloween.* Austin, Tex.: Raintree Steck-Vaughn, 1997.

Kindersley, Anabel. *Celebrations.* New York: DK Publishing, 1997.

Stevens, Kathryn. *Halloween Jack-O'-Lanterns.* Chanhassen, Minn.: Child's World, 1999.

Internet Sites

Halloween

http://wilstar.com/holidays/hallown.htm

Halloween: Myths, Monsters and Devils

http://www.illusions.com/halloween/hallows.htm

The History of Halloween

http://www.historychannel.com/halloween